HOW TO DO IT SERIES: No. 18

DESIGNING FOR THE STAGE

1. Model of setting for " The Taming of the Shrew " at the New Theatre, 1938.

Frontispiece

DESIGNING

for the

STAGE

DORIS ZINKEISEN

THE STUDIO: LONDON AND NEW YORK

First published . . October, 1938.
Reprinted . . . May, 1945.

"HOW TO DO IT" SERIES

Others in preparation.

Reg. U.S.

STUDIO

Pat. Off.

Printed in England by Hazell, Watson & Viney, Limited, London and Aylesbury. Published in London by The Studio Ltd., 66, Chandos Place, W.C.2, and in New York by The Studio Publications Inc., 381 Fourth Avenue.

CONTENTS

ILLUSTRATIONS

INTRODUCTION

The art of designing costumes and scenes for the stage is of so varied a nature that research and study are essential. Ever since the theatre cast off the conventionalism which, originating from the days of Egypt, Greece and Rome, persisted until well into the Victorian epoch, the stage designer has acquired endless opportunities ; but with these have come enormous responsibilities also.

This little book is not intended for those experienced in theatrical design, but it represents an attempt to explain the elements to those whose interest in the subject exceeds their knowledge.

So much depends upon the attitude of mind which the designer brings to bear upon the problems that confront him. For instance, there is often a great temptation to get carried away by some idea for a scene that may not be suitable to the play or may have no relation to it at all. These inspirations are the cause of many a disaster. Such scenes, however beautiful, are the equivalent of a bad piece of miscasting, and are no credit to the designer.

The most important feature in designing a scene successfully is that it should conform to all the requirements of the action of the play and be completely suitable both in planning and colour to create the right atmosphere. That is why it is so essential to read the play, hear the music, see the dances, and get thoroughly acquainted with the author's or composer's conception, in order that each scene shall receive every consideration as to suitability of treatment. Designers must endeavour to carry the play with them in every stroke of the brush.

There have been many words of advice written on how to get wonderful effects with twopennyworth of butter muslin and an old second-hand wing which only needs repainting. Such effects may be charming and the result will probably be stupendous, but such advice is crushing and worthless to budding designers. Whether you are designing a set for a gay carnival in a musical comedy, or a dungeon in the bitterest tragedy, your scene is acting a part and should be inspired like the player before appearing in front of an audience.

A scene should be planned with a flourish of trumpets. Let all the extravagant, ambitious ideas that have been piling up since reading the script of the play be concentrated, unhampered by the "butter muslin" outlook, on creating something that fulfils every one of your ideas.

The size of the funds at one's disposal may in some cases mean a curtailing of expenditure and a process of elimination must be gone through. Ingenuity and invention must be brought to bear in an effort to keep the design as near as possible to its original idea, having due regard to economy. Clever elimination in order to comply with circumstances will always retain most of your "splendid" scene, but to start with a rather wretched conception, making additions should funds permit, will inevitably leave traces of the original mediocre and parsimonious outlook which is to be avoided on the stage.

CHAPTER 1   THE STAGE

I must confess that I have a strong leaning towards the old-fashioned theatre—the auditorium overloaded with rather swirling ornate decoration, the boxes a welter of garlands, cupids and red plush drapery. The proscenium is generally terrific in its glitter of gold and ornamentation mounting up to a glory of more cupids and almost invariably crowned with a pair of flying ladies blowing coach horns on either side of a more dignified seated lady, with rather richer curves, who is entrusted with the important duty of holding the masks of Tragedy and Comedy.

This kind of decoration seems a far truer atmosphere for a theatre than the cold unyielding interior of some modern playhouses. Architects and interior decorators to-day seem, when entrusted with designing a theatre, to disregard completely the fact that it is a house of entertainment and that the moment an audience enter a theatre they should be made conscious of feelings of suppressed excitement and anticipation before the curtain goes up.

Theatres should be decorated with a view to creating this atmosphere and should not look like the interior of some large hotel, without any of the glamour and artificial gaiety so abundantly prevailing in the work of those bygone decorators, and I am certain that it is possible to preserve this spirit of the theatre in decoration and architecture, while employing modern treatment.

Before embarking on the ways and means of designing a setting I want to introduce the potential stage designer to a bare empty stage.

To one standing in the auditorium and looking from a sea of stalls covered in dust-sheets, the stage will probably be lit only by a working light or a small section of the footlights—a huge gaping mouth—a picture by Gustave Doré—full of dark corners, with a general aroma of musty glue and dust but nevertheless strangely exciting.

The proscenium of each theatre varies in its size of opening ; *Pro-* and this is a very important measurement for the setting of all *scenium* scenes, in order that the line of sight from every seat should be correct ; in other words, so that everybody in the audience has a good view of the stage. Riots have been started in the pit and gallery by irate playgoers who have had their favourite cut off from sight by a piece of scenery. I shall go into this question of sight later.

Act Drop or House Tabs The Floats

The Act Drop or House Tabs (Tableaux)—as the curtain is called—are just inside the proscenium arch. The floats or footlights are on the auditorium side of the curtain and they illuminate it during the overture—a very exciting moment on a first night—and play an important part in the general lighting effect. While on this subject, it is interesting to recall that, before curtains were thought of, various devices were employed by the management to distract the audience's attention while the simple scene changes of the time were in progress. Lights and mirrors were flashed, a sudden blast blown on horns, or—surely most efficacious of all—a commotion was deliberately started at the back of the theatre !

Boat-truck

A " boat-truck " is constructed as part of a rostrum and has a set of small squat wheels let in underneath which will enable all rather cumbersome pieces of scenery to slide easily across the stage into position.

Occasionally an entire little scene is mounted on a boat-truck ; or it may be a flat in which there is a rather elaborate and heavy fireplace. Boat-trucks are also used for objects that actually move across the stage during a scene, such as a ship leaving a pier, etc.

Back-cloths

" Backcloths " are made of canvas and have a batten at the top and roller at the bottom. They vary in height and length according to the size of scene.

Borders

" Borders " are also of canvas and vary in depth. A very intricate design that has an exceptionally uneven outline or a tree border of branches and leaves, which is often a rather lacy affair, is always " netted out." The net is used to keep all the loose pieces of canvas in place without being apparent from the front. Some borders are " battened out," which means that they are framed out at the back. Occasionally it is necessary to have tails on a border for " masking in " at the side. This type of border is made very much longer each end than it is in the centre.

There are many things individual to every production that are made by the scene builder ; all I have described are the chief parts that are used in every show to make a scene.

Front Cloth

A front cloth generally hangs anywhere between No. 1 or No. 2 electric lighting battens. As a rule it measures the full width of

2. Model stage showing revolve, false proscenium, and tormentors.

the proscenium and is masked in at the sides by the proscenium wings. The productions in which a front cloth is used most are often revue, pantomime, musical comedy and turns in variety.

Cut cloths are used in place of wings and borders. Sometimes the canvas is cut to the required outline and a net used if the outline is particularly intricate as in the borders of that type, or an alternative is to batten out a cut cloth on a framework.

Gauze can be used most effectively. It is actually very coarse cotton net and can be had in several colours. A gauze hung directly behind the false proscenium or proscenium wings will add a softening appearance to a scene.

Where it is necessary to produce a mist or thick fog on the stage grey gauzes are used one behind the other until the right density of atmosphere is achieved. A scene of this sort lit properly can look most realistic. To give the idea of the fog clearing, the gauzes are taken up one by one.

Another way gauze is used, probably the most spectacular of all, is when it has a design painted on it. This design will only show up when the gauze is lighted from in front, making it appear as solid as a painted cloth. Directly the lighting comes in behind it the gauze, with its design, fades away, revealing the scene which has been set behind.

When the curtain is up, directly inside the proscenium are the tormentors. In the old days these tormentors used to have doors which were used as entrances. They were part of the proscenium and built with just the same solidity. Nowadays they are part of the scenery, and the entrances, if any, have curtains in place of the doors. Above each entrance is a small square hole through which the electrician may direct his perch lights.

In order to frame a scene or to close in the aperture to certain required proportions another small proscenium, called a " false proscenium," is very often used. This is generally covered in the same material or painted the same as the tormentors and always stands at the same angle as does the main proscenium. In the case of some productions a false proscenium is impracticable. For example, where there are many scenes which vary in size, it will be necessary to close the opening for a small scene, whereas the next scene on the programme might be a large full set and the opening should expand again. For this purpose proscenium wings and borders are most useful. The borders can be lowered or taken up and the wings can be adjusted to any required size of opening by moving them off or on stage. Behind the border is the bridge, a swinging platform, *The* which can also be adjusted for height. This bridge carries lamps *Bridge* which are used to " spot " any part of the scene or to be directed on to any of the characters, following their movements.

The " flies " are where everything hangs. You look up and see, *The* suspended dangerously above your head, great heavy electric *Flies* lighting battens, backcloths, borders, sets of flats battened together, ceilings folded up—a tangle of ropes ; and yet no matter how impossibly full it appears to be up there, a master carpenter will always say that there is plenty of room for more !

Each piece of scenery that hangs has three sets of lines by which *Lines* it is lowered into position or taken up again. These are known as short line, centre line and long line and are always knotted to whatever they carry. To prevent these lines from fouling each other when not in use, a small sandbag is attached to the end of each.

Above the flies is the grid, away up in the roof, which supports *The* all the pulleys and their lines for everything that is hanging from *Grid* the flies. On either side of the stage is a gallery from which everything in the flies can be worked, sometimes by counter-weights, though more often by brawn and muscle. These galleries are known as the " fly floor " and occasionally they are *The Fly* joined by a third gallery running along the back wall, although *Floor* the shape of most London theatres forbids this.

The switchboard for controlling all the electrical installation is worked from the " fly floor " in most theatres, though I have known it to be most inconveniently placed in the prompt corner.

Prompt and O.P. (opposite prompt) sides of the stage are very *Prompt* important stage directions to remember. The prompt side is stage *& O.P.* left, which means when standing on the stage facing the auditorium it is on the left side. The prompt corner is the quarter deck of the stage manager. All his switches, bells and telephones to all parts of the house are there for him to control everything while the performance is in progress and, with his eyes glued to the prompt copy of the play, he—or his assistant—is ready with the cue should any of the cast forget their lines.

13

He rings the curtain up or down by pressing a button and very often has to act a part in the play into the bargain.

On all stages just in a line with the bottom of the act drop or directly behind it is the carpet cut. This is a long cut in the floor of the stage reaching very nearly the full width of the proscenium opening and is covered by a hinged flap. After laying a stage cloth, the untidy edge is tucked into the carpet cut and the flap replaced, leaving it all neat. The stage may also have other cuts or bridges, generally towards the back or " up stage." These bridges vary in width and, unlike the carpet cut, are not worked with a flap but can be lowered like a lift right down underneath the stage.

Sometimes in quayside scenes or on board ship when someone gradually disappears descending a flight of stone steps or a companionway, he is in reality disappearing down one of these cuts and away underneath the stage.

In pantomime where demons shoot up through the floor this is either through a star trap, which is in the shape of a star opening upwards, or through an ordinary trap with two flaps also opening upwards. The demon sits waiting for his cue on a little platform underneath the stage and at the given word is shot up through the flaps, which immediately fall back into place again, and it all appears to have been done by magic.

A revolving stage or turntable—the idea of which originally came from Japan—is not fitted to all theatres, though it is quite possible to fit one temporarily if required without tearing up the whole flooring of the stage. A temporary revolve can be placed, complete, right on to the existing stage, and is generally about a foot in depth, so remember that this brings everything that stands on it at least a foot above the level of the actual stage.

With a revolving stage there is a tremendous advantage. It will turn in either direction, and for quick changes, as may be imagined, it proves invaluable. While the one scene is being played another can be set, or part of it set, in readiness to be moved round into position. The plan should be that the big scenes fit perfectly in with the little scenes and these big scenes can, if necessary, encroach on more than the true half of the circular revolve, being thus as large and impressive as may be necessary. This is often a very troublesome business as little

5. A bookbacking, showing 3-ply edge.

4. The same built door from the correct side.

3. A built door lined and cleated into a flat (note the weight and brace supporting the flat).

6. A plan of the revolving stage showing the positions of the two scenes, as they set in relation to one another.

A   The gallows.   Being hinged to the scene they may be folded round on to the revolve in readiness to be opened out as they are on the plan when the scene is moved into position.

B   The Backcloth.   Before the revolve can move round to the next scene the backcloth must be taken up or flown.

C   The dotted lines indicate the positions of each border to be used in the first scene. As the revolve moves round for the second scene these borders will be taken up.

D   The Wall.   This portion of the wall and gate-post being just overlapping, the revolve comes round into position.

E   The House Row.   This ground row, like the wall, is partly off the revolve.   The portion extending beyond the edge of the revolve joins up by lines and cleats to the main portion when it comes into position.

CURTAIN

A

HINGED

A

CURTAIN

HINGED

BORDER

FRONT OF CEILING

Act I Scene I

CEILING HINGED TO BACK FLAT

PELMET

BLIND

DUMMY WINDOW

SIDE BORDER

No 2 P.S. WING

No 1 R.S. WING

WALL

D

DOOR

WALL

SET PIECE A.

GREEN HOUSE

HOUSE

STEPS UP

BACKING

ROSTRUM 2FT HIGH

DOOR

PORCH

O.P. HOUSE RETURN

No 1 O.P.

OPENING

Act I. Scene 2.

B

E

BACK CLOTH.

HOUSE ROW.

B

C SKY BORDER

C SKY BORDER

C SKY BORDER

SIDE BORDER

TRAILER CURTAINS

FALSE PROS

PROSCENIUM OPENING.

₵

SCALE IN FEET.

0 1 2 3 4 5 6 7 8 9 10 11 12 13 14 15 16 17 18 19 20 21 22 23 24 25 26 27 28 29 30

17

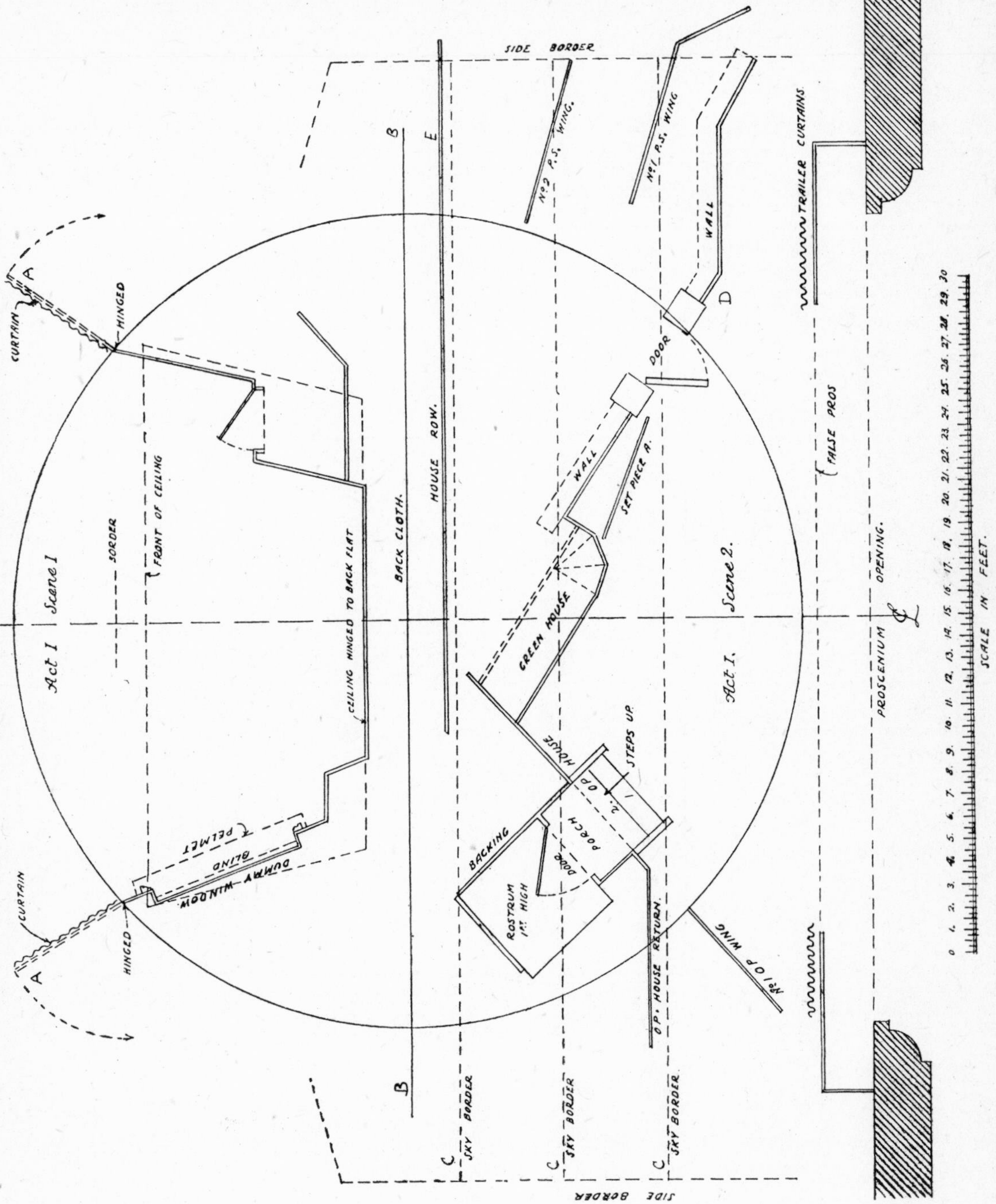

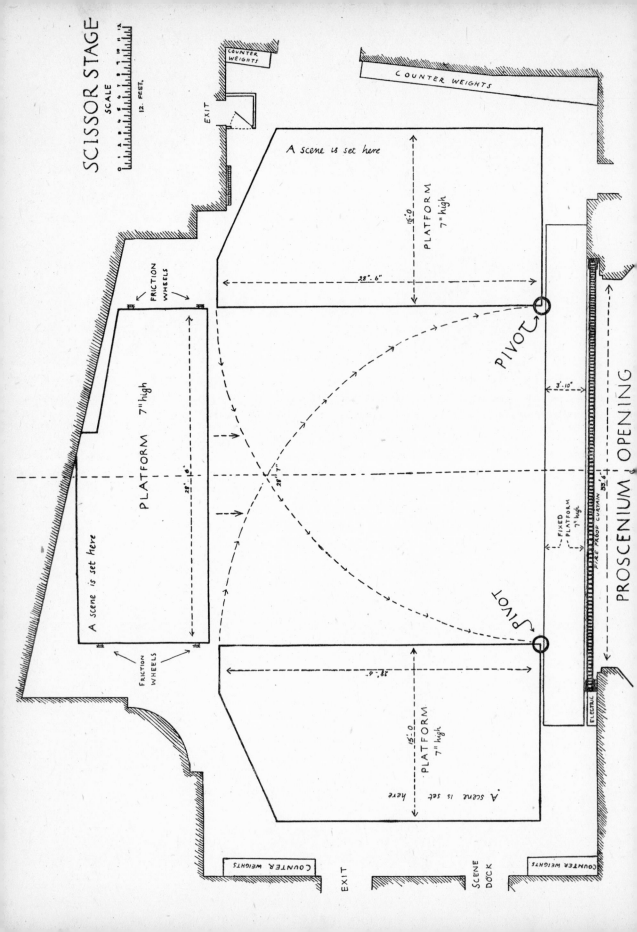

scenes take up a lot more room than one thinks. It is important to remember that any scenery on the revolve should be set at least six to eight inches within the edge, as otherwise it may either get swept off or foul something while turning round. Though a revolving stage can be so advantageous, it is also full of pitfalls and snags which will give rise to many nightmares or sleepless nights. I cannot attempt to describe such *contretemps* because they have a strange way of cropping up in the most unexpected and tantalising manner and all designers must put up with it. The result often is that one's favourite scene has to be re-designed because the quick change has to be made somehow and the "favourite" always seems to be one that can most conveniently go to the wall.

There is another type of stage used for quick changes that is *Scissor* called a "scissor stage." It is divided into three separate tables, *Stage* enabling an entire scene to be set on each one ready to come before the curtain. There is one on either side of the stage and one in the centre. The prompt and O.P. side tables are situated up and down stage and swing round into position on a pivot while the centre one stands right at the back or up stage and slides down in a straight line into place. These tables are 7 in. in thickness and generally about 14 ft. deep. In order that the side tables can pass the centre one as they pivot round, the corner must be cut off, which may, at times, hamper the setting possibilities and rather confines a scissor stage to a certain type of production. For interior scenes that need not be very large scissor stages are perfect, but a stage 14 ft. deep is of no use to a dance producer with a chorus of twenty-four to thirty-six girls and boys or a choreographer directing a ballet.

Sometimes to obtain a little deeper stage the centre table, which is straight across the back, may have a flap attached to it after it has moved down and away from the back wall, though any scenery that stands on this flap can be set only after the table has moved into position, which naturally reduces the quickness of the change.

Before leaving the stage take a look at the shape of the actual *The* wall all round. Sometimes the construction is such that it will *Wall* restrict certain rather deep scenes. Walls occasionally come out at strange angles and limit the amount of space at one's disposal. Always have a ground plan of the stage with the positions of anything awkward in the way of constructions marked very clearly.

Opposite : 7. Plan of scissor stage.

Flats

" Flats " are the basis of most scenes where large expanses require to be built. They vary in length and width and their height is governed by the height of the proscenium border. The most usual heights are 18 ft., 20 ft. and 24 ft. The width can be anything from 1 ft. to 8 ft., but anything beyond that is rather difficult to handle.

The construction of a flat consists of stiles and rails, mortised in the corner, and the centre rails affixed by a shoe. The whole is finally canvassed over. Flats are held together in two ways, either by hinging them or by lines and cleats, but it is possible to hinge them only when they are to fold inwards. If, for example, the scene is an interior where there are several fairly large expanses of wall, it is probably to your advantage to hinge the flats together, in which case the entire surface may be canvassed over without untidy joins ; where hinging can be arranged it is always better. There are many places where it is absolutely necessary to line and cleat flats, such as an angle outwards.

Doors

All flats are kept in position on the stage by braces and weights. Where a door comes into the centre of a flat the wooden construction is reinforced, leaving the aperture that is to be occupied by the door and reinforced again at the bottom with an iron sill. A framework of wide moulding round the face always gives a good finish to a doorway. The door and the reveal are built in one, ready to be lined and cleated to the flat when it is being set. Doors are sometimes real ones made like those in any house, but very often it is necessary that they should be light, in which case they are frames canvassed over and painted.

Windows

Windows are constructed much as the real ones and are fitted into the flat in the same manner as the doors. When the designs call for a lattice window black tape is used to give the effect of the leaded diamond or square panes.

Backings & Book-backings

All backings to doors, etc., are small replicas of flats—sometimes singly or sometimes hinged together. A " bookbacking " is two small flats hinged together which will open out at any angle for setting. Bookbackings are used to mask in a door, fireplace or any

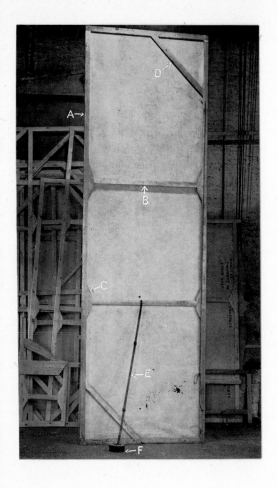

9. A flat to take a door.

8. A flat.

 A Stile.
 B Rail.
 C Shoe or toggle.
 D Batten.
 E Brace.
 F Weight.

Stage scenery is made mostly with flats. This photograph shows a flat on the reverse side, and the brace and weight supporting it. The brace hooks into a large screw eye in the rail of the flat.

kind of opening and need only be high and wide enough for the
purpose.

Wings

Wings are constructed very like flats except where the contour
of the design is varied and uneven. If, for example, the design
of the wing happened to call for trees or a building with a number
of parapets or mouldings making the outline irregular, to the
already existing stiles and rails there would be the addition of
sufficient three-ply wood to allow for the outline. The whole
wing is then canvassed over, including the three-ply, ready for the
scene painter who, after he has finished his work on it, will mark
out the correct contours carefully in bright blue. This serves as a
guide to the scene builder when he cuts out the outline with his
fretsaw.

Book-
wings

A " bookwing " is on the same principle as a bookbacking and
is hinged together in two parts opening out to the required angle.

Ground
Rows

" Ground rows " are all heights and lengths. The smaller ones
are mostly built of three-ply wood as they generally represent some
subject that will require cutting out, such as distant hills with trees,
a hedge, a wall—even a crowd of people—in fact, any rather
lengthy bit of scenery that is cut out and set by itself on the stage.
The three-ply is reinforced at the back with a light framework, or
" battened out." In larger and more solid ground rows, however,
canvas constructions and battening out is generally used with just
enough three-ply to cut out any outline necessary.

Set
Pieces

" Set pieces " are made in the same way as ground rows. They
are single objects that are set by themselves, such as a shrub, a
figure or small group of figures, a tree or perhaps two trees
together. All set pieces are held in position by braces and weights.

Rostrum

Anything that is to carry weight of any description has to be
built on a rostrum even if it stands only a foot above stage level.
Such constructions are often built to be collapsible, which is sometimes very necessary with the limited space for packing away at
the back of most stages. A rostrum when being set on the stage
is opened out, the top is put on, and disguising bits of scenery
arranged round make it into a mountain, the upper story of a
house, or perhaps just that part of a flight of stairs which terminates off stage. When very large built structures have to be set in
a quick change it is often best to have them built on a " boat-truck."

22

10. A rostrum.

11. Flight of steps
showing construction.

CHAPTER 3 TYPES OF SETTINGS

In early discussions between producer and designer the arranging of scenes to the best advantage in order that there shall be no long waits between the changes always presents a most difficult problem. We are still in the Dark Ages when it comes to the shifting of scenery, in spite of all the advancements of to-day.

Modern theatres spring up from time to time bristling with the latest devices which never seem to extend as far as the stage ; and so far no stage has appeared with equipment equal to the demands created by the lightning changes of scene required by so many present-day productions. Too long a pause coming at an ill-timed moment in a play may do irretrievable harm to an important sequence or cause an audience to falter in their interest. To avoid starting on an idea that may prove impracticable all scenes should be visualised with a view to setting and striking.

Productions with a great number of scenes will have to be planned so that large full-stage settings and small inset or medium scenes dovetail into one another, and arranged for these changes to be effected to eliminate the danger of long waits.

Small scenes will be set right down stage, giving the larger sets ample time for setting behind them while the performance is in progress. These small scenes are constructed with a view to striking them very quickly and they may consist of as few as three flats hinged together that can be folded and flown in a few seconds.

One is not always in such difficulties with large productions, and there is occasionally an opportunity to use sets of curtains, which are of considerable assistance during changes of scene, especially when they are used as the background for song or dance numbers, giving more time for setting behind.

There are many types of production, each one requiring a different mode of staging : plays, serious or otherwise, musical plays, musical comedy, operetta, ballet, revue, opera and panto-mime.

Revue is a type of production in which curtains can be used most frequently, offering great scope for displaying creative ability and beautiful materials in curtain design. There is no place in revue

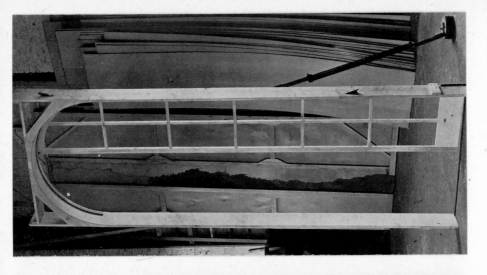

14. A window.

13. A canvassed door.

12. Bookbacking (hinged to open like a book).

for anything that appears to be merely utilitarian. When curtains are employed they should be as much a part of the beauty of the show as any setting or costume and should never be regarded as something that is merely closing in on the previous scene for the sake of convenience. In revue one is given more chances of showing versatility in stage design than in any other type of production, for revue should be the epitome of beauty, charm, comedy and audacity in the design of its costumes and settings, always tempered with wit.

Plays do not usually demand large numbers of scenes and seldom present many difficulties in setting or striking. In cases where there are two or three scenes in one act these may be arranged to set one behind the other and most of the scenery constructed to fly when the time comes for striking it.

Shakespearian plays, in which there are always numerous scenes, were originally acted on a bare stage. They are open to almost any treatment ranging from the traditional to the fantastic, but, as they are written, none of the plays allows for waits between the scenes and to permit such waits would prove extremely detrimental to the continuity. One way of surmounting this is to design a series of scenes that can be set on the revolve or scissor stage. A momentary blackout is all that is required to enable the stage to come into position with the next scene. Another way of dealing with this problem of many scenes is to have a single setting which remains on the stage during the whole performance, designed in a way that allows for interchangeable sections to be used as a means of altering the scene.

Pantomime is full of complications such as transformation scenes, fairies flying and demons appearing. The atmosphere of magic prevailing in pantomimes must be maintained at all costs and ingenious contrivances invented to produce the necessary quota of gasps of astonishment each Christmas.

A transformation scene was in the old days the *pièce de résistance* of the show. Both children and grown-ups got a tremendous thrill when the Ogre's awful cave full of bones and terrifying creatures was suddenly transformed into the beautiful palace of the Fairy Prince. The scene was planned in the most ingenious way, as the complete transformation took place before the audience, in most

26

15. A ground row.

Ground rows are all heights and lengths. The smaller ones are mostly
built of three-ply wood as they generally represent some subject that
will require cutting out, such as distant hills with trees, a hedge, a wall—
even a crowd of people—in fact any rather lengthy bit of scenery that is
cut out and set by itself on the stage.

cases accompanied by a blinding flash which prevented one from seeing anything for a few seconds. To change from the Ogre's cave to the Prince's Palace each ugly piece of scenery had to disappear, leaving the beautiful piece in its place.

When cut cloths and borders were used the new one would be dropped down in front of the old or the old one taken up, revealing the new. Ground rows would appear up through the stage while the old ground row disappeared and for this effect the cuts or bridges in the stage would be used. Flats or wings would be constructed so that they had an additional half that worked on the principle of a leaf in a book, being painted both sides, and to make the change the centre leaf section was pulled round by means of an invisible wire attached to it.

Gauzes were often used very effectively and made to disappear with an alteration in lighting. These are simple changes to give an idea of what takes place, but in the old Drury Lane panto-mimes there seemed no end to the marvels of staging appearances and disappearances.

Pantomime to-day is a very dull affair, entirely lacking in any of the spectacular and remarkable feats of stagecraft that always made that traditional Christmas show so wonderful and exciting. There is no excitement in a modern pantomime. The last of it seemed to have gone with the late Julian Wylie. And all too rarely do we see to-day a harlequinade, that last remaining link with the stage of Grimaldi.

CH: 4   DESIGNING A SETTING

The overture to making a model should be a very large scribbling pad on which endless little rough pencil sketches can be made.

Side by side with these sketches make a rough ground plan. Disappointment is often the result of preparing a beautifully finished sketch which when made into a model may be found to have lost all its charm owing to certain rearrangements and adjustments that alter the composition in order to make it practical for the stage.   Ground plans are always full of cold hard truths and are the best way, in the early preparation stages, to find out what is workable and what is not.

It is essential to have a small model stage, which provides a very satisfactory means of judging proportions, by setting up a scene, or even parts of a scene in preparation ; a very good idea is immediately given of what the full-size effect will eventually be.

This little model stage should be made to a scale of half-inch to the foot, which is the usual scale for all stage designs, and it can be of a size that is average among theatres.   The proscenium opening of most theatres is anything from 28 ft. to 36 ft. across and in the model it will be quite simple to adjust this according to the measurement required to coincide with the theatre in question, though for exceptional theatres like Covent Garden or the Coliseum such a proscenium opening would be very much too small.

This model should have a working section in the centre representing a revolving stage, which will probably be necessary for quick changes. These can all be tried in preparation on the model revolve to ensure that everything works as it should, thus avoiding disasters later.

There are two struts in the corners opposite the proscenium, and they support a rail on either side that represents the flies from which all cloths or borders will hang.

Let us imagine that all preliminary discussions with the producer and anyone else concerned with the arrangements of the stage and designs have been settled, the theatre decided upon and the approximate date of opening provisionally fixed.   Have the ground plan of the theatre pinned up in a prominent place so that measurements may be taken easily.

Start work on the model with an adequate supply of white cardboard or very thick cartridge paper, a good-sized glue pot that should be kept simmering to be ready for use at any moment, a scale rule, a strong knife which is very sharp and also a small pointed knife. If you happen to know a surgeon get him to pass on to you his sharp little scalpel blades, which are far the best knives for modelling. You will also need some sharp scissors, large and small, a small saw and a fairly extensive variety of poster colours. All dimensions must be absolutely correct, as this model, when it is completed, will be handed to the scene builder to work from; and no contractor can be held responsible for his scenes being of wrong proportions unless all measurements given to him are strictly accurate.

We are assuming that the proscenium opening of the theatre is 36 ft. We will imagine the production is one that will depend on quick changes so that it is necessary to make use of the revolving stage.

The first set is found to be the villa of an elderly lady living in North Oxford. Her niece, who lives with her during the holidays, is an attractive young person at a finishing school for young ladies at Lausanne. Obviously for this scene something should be discovered about the architecture in the residential part of North Oxford. The type of building, on examination, is about as hideous as anything described as architecture can be—mid-Victorian, pseudo-Gothic.

The author has supplied us with a splendid opportunity to start this comedy with a rather flippant caricature of a very ordinary scene, which shows a garden and the back of the house, with a door leading outwards. There is the usual conservatory—impossible to imagine any garden in North Oxford without its greenhouse. A high wall with black iron spikes as a protection against burglars or little boys runs across the back of the stage, a gate leads to the road and more wall continues down towards the prompt corner. Behind the wall there is a row of equally dreadful villas that appear to be on the opposite side of the road. All these villas have the same pointed gables ornamented by wooden eaves tormented with travesties of Gothic design. They are built of every conceivable shade of brick that is ugly, and decorated by ornamental brickwork in contrasting colours. The house is stage right and is placed at an angle bringing the door into a good position for the characters to " make an entrance "—

17. Completed model of the " North Oxford " scene.

33

been marked as a replica of the ground plan. Each part can be glued by a strip of the cardboard that has been left on the bottom purposely for attachment. The backcloth will need to have a slat of wood attached across the top in order that it may rest on the two rails of the model that represent the flies. The borders are fixed in the same way as the cloth and their positions must be determined according to the line of sight in the theatre as they must mask in the flies.

We will assume that as each piece of the model took its shape in cardboard it was also thought of in terms of scenery, but for the purpose of making everything clear this point is being separately dealt with.

Flats are used in most cases where the subject requires building in large flat areas. In constructing our house three flats will be necessary. The straight area measuring 12 ft. will consist of two flats hinged together ; if it were made in one piece it would be too large to be moved about easily and quickly. There will also be a " return," an 8-ft. flat which is lined and cleated to the others forming the side of the house. The carpenter's working drawings will show how these flats are constructed, the shaded part being the three-ply wood that is added in order to cut out the contours of the roof and round the edge of the doorway.

There are two steps up to the doorway. These steps will be made of timber, the usual size for any stairs or steps on the stage being 6-in. rises and 9-in. treads. Two steps up bring the entrance to the house 1 ft. above stage level and entail the use of a small rostrum, which extends from the doorway into the house, measuring 7 ft. in length.

The porch and door into the house will be a backing which need not be more than 11 ft. high, as this will be sufficient for the purpose of masking in. This consists of the doorpiece measuring 4 ft. with two 2-ft. returns on either side, all three being hinged together. The door opens off stage as can be seen on the ground plan. Whenever doors appear, always indicate on the ground plan whether they are to open off stage or on stage. Behind the door is a bookbacking.

The conservatory is set separately and is made collapsible. In the working drawings a good idea is given of how each part is made and hinged so that the whole conservatory can be set quickly. The back is just a framework " A " with a section of three-ply for cutting out the ornamentation along the top of the roof. The roof itself is a light framework, the three wedge-shaped sections being hinged together and the whole thing canvassed over " B." The side of the conservatory is made in the same way with small sections hinged together forming the counterpart of the fan-shaped part of the roof " C."

The roof is hinged along the back framework " A " just immediately below the three-ply ornamentation, hanging flat when not being used and opened out to rest on the supporting sides when set.

The walls and gate are a ground row. The wall section is a framework canvassed with the iron railings cut out in three-ply. The piers on either side of the gate are also framework canvassed with the caps framed correctly out in three-ply wood to make the contour. The gate itself is entirely made of three-ply wood on a light framework and subsequently canvassed for painting, the iron spikes being made of timber and let into slots between the framework. The wall and gate will be set in two separate halves. From the conservatory to the end of the gate, which comes on to the revolve, the second portion will be set ready to move on to the revolve the moment it comes into position.

The villas behind the wall are another ground row, measuring 31 ft. by 15 ft., and constructed very much on the lines of the house, though with a rather lighter framework. The section that sets on the revolve can be hinged together, but the last 10 ft. must be run on after the revolve is in position and then be lined and cleated up to the larger section.

The main purpose of the two wings on the prompt side is to mask in that side of the stage, but their designs of another villa and a small tree surrounded by an iron railing help to give the over-populated feeling of North Oxford. On the O.P. side there is one single wing that represents a portion of the house.

The set pieces (bushes, shrubs, etc.) are small and mostly three-ply.

The backcloth for this setting will need to be 44 ft. by 27 ft. There is a good expanse of sky and a prospect of many roofs and spires between the tree-tops. The two borders represent billowy clouds. These are cut to the shape of each billow and make a somewhat more amusing finish to a rather flippant scene than the usual straight line of a blue sky border.

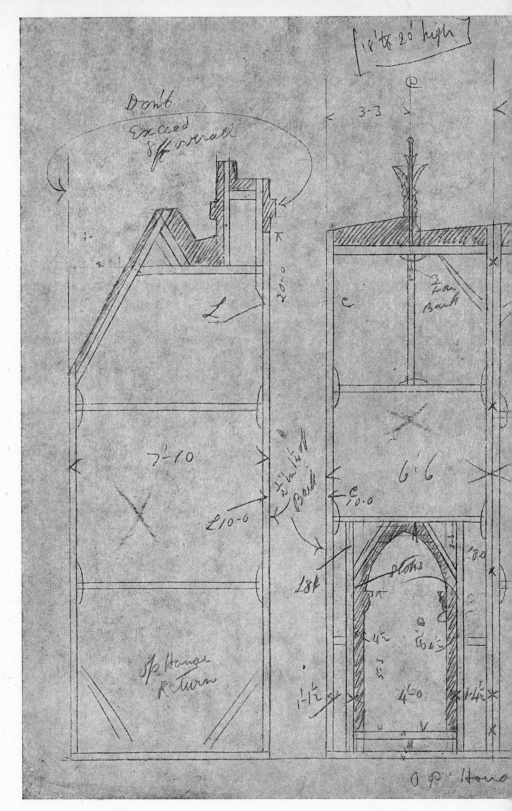

18. Carpenter's plan of part of

As the work progresses, the portions completed are marked off by big re
shaded lines s

use of the " North Oxford " scene.

...cil crosses.   The small crosses indicate where hinges are required.   The
...ere three-ply is used.

Back to back with this garden in North Oxford is set a little bedroom in the school at Lausanne. This must be a small, rather simple scene. The walls are plain. In the centre facing the auditorium there is a bed which has long white spotted muslin curtains with frills. The window is on the prompt side and also has white spotted curtains very much draped across. The dressing-table has a flounce of the same material and the rest of the furniture in the room is white with a painted design typical of Switzerland.

This set consists entirely of 18-ft. flats. For the purpose of a quick change, the ceiling will have to be attached to the back flat so that both may be flown at the same time. The back flat and the ceiling are hinged together, and when not in use are folded in two. To set them, they are lowered on to the stage. Three lines are attached to grummets (or loops) on the front of the ceiling by which it is then raised at first higher than it will eventually be in order to leave sufficient space to set the rest of the flats forming the room. These having been placed in position, the ceiling is lowered on to the top of the flats.

On the O.P. side of the stage there is a door that is set in a flat facing the auditorium. The door opens on stage and has a bookbacking behind it that might be the end of a passage. As it is so necessary to preserve the idea of the room being very small, one has to resort to all kinds of tricks in order to give enough space for the action and the necessary number of people on the stage.

Having taken the light blue flats down to the edge of the revolve, giving the scene a depth of 11 ft. 6 in. to keep the illusion of smallness, it is necessary to have a gallows of black velvet, which consists of arms shaped like a gallows in structure that are hinged to the blue flat to fold in flush with the flat itself and which swing out and extend to the required angle when the revolve is in position.

The proscenium wings being also of black velvet merge and make a rather deeper frame, at the same time helping to keep the idea of a small room without constricting the acting space.

The blind and curtains over the window are the responsibility of the property master, and he fixes these both permanently on the flat.

The bed curtains are on a separate bracket that fits into a socket on the back flat.

CHAPTER 5   LIGHTING

Lighting is just as individual a matter as the use of colour in the designs for a scene or costumes, and one cannot attempt to give guidance in such matters, which must be left to the designer himself in conjunction with the producer. It may, however, be of assistance to indicate certain broad principles.

There are certain scenes which can be designed with a view to using strong lighting to obtain dramatic effect. For instance, the scene shows a courtyard by moonlight. The buildings are white and cast strong shadows. If they are painted in such a way as to take half the weight off the shoulders of the lighting it is possible to retain a great deal more of the true picture than by having to flood the stage with some sinister mixture of blues and greens to get the effect, at the same time endeavouring to keep enough light to distinguish the characters.

Very strong light in any colour other than white always plays havoc with all scenes and costumes unless they have been designed in colours to counteract such drastic treatment, so that in scenes where such lighting effects are inevitable it is very advisable to experiment first with all colours used in both scene and costumes.

The lighting equipment in most theatres consists of floats or footlights which are generally divided into sections of blue, red and amber lights. These can be brought in separately or with all three colours at once. They are also divided into the prompt side, centre and O.P. side sections that may be used apart or together.

Like the rest of the electrical equipment the floats can be faded in or out on what is known as a "dimmer." When the floats are in, their effect is to give a general flooding of light over the stage, thrown rather upwards and catching the figures and faces of the actors but leaving the ground unlighted.

The lighting battens hanging in the flies will illuminate this blackened ground and also the top of anything else standing on the stage, as their light is directed down at an angle and facing slightly up stage.

In the average-sized theatre there are four or five of these lighting battens, and they are numbered as they go back. No. 1

batten is right down stage just a foot or two from the false proscenium and usually lights the first border. No. 2 batten is about four feet up stage of No. 1, and so they go back. These battens, like the floats, have sections of red, blue and amber, and for some productions it may be necessary to have a larger proportion of one colour than of another.

The bridge hangs directly behind the false proscenium, and is fitted with lamps that will swivel round into any position required. There is a man in charge of each lamp whose business it is to follow the actor he is "spotting." Apart from spotting, these lamps may be used for the purpose of flooding some part of the scene and remain in that case stationary during the whole of that period.

In order to change the colour of the light a gelatine slide is slipped into the lamp. These gelatines are made in every shade and colour, and are used extensively for all lights including the arcs or half-watt lamps that are used on the stage itself. A stage spot lamp is on an adjustable standard and may be placed anywhere in the wings and directed wherever a "flood" is needed. There is generally another group of lamps in the front of the house. Sometimes they are ranged round the balustrade of the dress circle, but more often only at the back of the gallery. They are very strong arc lamps and used mainly for spotting the actors, and, apart from the floats, are the only means of lighting anyone who is playing or speaking below the false proscenium.

The perch arcs are directed through a small square aperture cut in the tormentors. They are used for spotting part of the scene or following the actors, though they are prevented from turning very far up stage by the sides of the tormentors cutting off the beam of light. These lamps are also provided with gelatine for colour changes. A "baby" spot can be put anywhere and at any angle on the stage, and is used in places where it is impossible to arrange any other type of lamp because of restrictions of space.

The electrician is also responsible for the light fittings that are used on the stage, such as chandeliers, brackets, table lamps, or fires that have to appear to be burning in grates.

40

20.　Costume for pantomime.

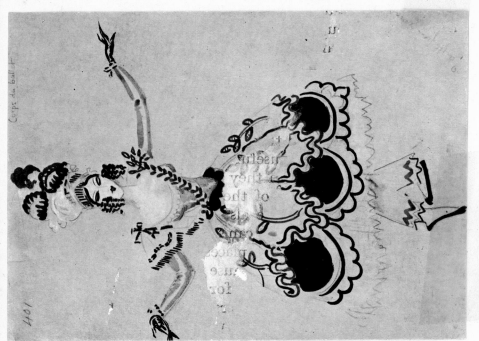

19.　Costume for ballet.

CHAPTER 6   PROPERTIES

Everything inside a scene comes under the heading of " props " —furniture, pictures on the walls, curtains or furnishing, carpets, mirrors, table appointments, food or drink, flowers, live-stock, ornaments, telephones, cigarettes, guns and babies (if they are not real ones).

The property room in a theatre is full of the strangest things, and the property master is constantly being asked to work miracles at short notice.

I remember when I designed the settings for " Oliver Twist " the bull terrier the property master procured for Bill Sikes was one of the finest specimens I have ever seen, but life in the property room between his appearances each evening, in spite of his daily exercise, aroused some latent savagery in his being far beyond that which was expected of him in his histrionic display, and this was not confined to performances. There was not a soul in the theatre he had not bitten, even the night watchman, who was found early one morning cowering up in the flies where he had spent most of the night after a desperate race for life round a dark theatre, vaulting stalls and piles of scenery, pursued by a very realistic " Bull's-eye."

Many things are made in the property room, and some property masters are extremely skilful at modelling articles in clay and casting them in papier mâché, or making pieces of furniture. But most important of all they must be intensely adept in the art of faking. Fake is the watchword of " props."

When any properties are being made from a design or drawing it is more satisfactory to be able to work from a design that is to scale, but, as a rule, the usual scale of half-inch to the foot is too small. For example, a mask would be impossible to make to so small a scale and would probably be best made from a drawing that was the actual size.

Properties that require delicate or specialised painting should be painted by the designer and, if necessary, made by him. The result is more likely to be nearer the intended idea.

Hand properties are things which any of the actors carry or are

21. Late eighteenth-century costumes for a Fair scene in Revue.

necessary to the part they are playing—for example, sticks or umbrellas, masks, wands, musical instruments, swords or anything small enough to handle easily. These properties are nearly always kept in the dressing-room by the person who has to use them, and are therefore in the care of his dresser.

Curtains for windows and chair coverings are nearly always made by a firm of upholsterers, and do not come into the hands of the property master until they are delivered ready to be used.

Where there are curtains on windows, over a bed, etc., the materials are selected by the designer from patterns, and in most cases a fairly large piece of the material should be seen before a final decision is made.

Always look at materials for the stage under an artificial light, as under these conditions most colours change very considerably, and even more so under the amber lighting that is used so often. Reds are the most deceptive of all, because they become more than three times as bright under artificial light. A velvet that appears black in daylight when submitted to the stage lighting changes to a rich claret. Dark reds go almost vermilion. Purples or violets must always be chosen with great care, as they will become too red immediately the artificial light is near them. Often to arrive at the shade of purple required on the stage it is necessary to select a material that is really almost blue. Blues are difficult in stage lighting, and unless a blue has quite a lot of green in it, it will become grey or mauve under the lights ; and, if it is dark blue, it will go black. Green is a fairly good colour for holding its own. Yellow is also good, unless it is too pale and loses everything, but all colours are subject to a certain amount of change in stage lighting and should be chosen accordingly.

A design for the shape of curtains and pelmets should be made, especially if they are to hang in any particular way or if the trimmings take any elaborate shape. Trimmings must all be chosen, and if there is a pattern to be *appliqué* or painted on the material, designs should be given to the upholsterer with careful instructions. Where a patterned material is to be used it is advisable to have a good-sized piece showing plenty of the repeat in order to try it on the stage. Sometimes a pattern will look nothing from the front and sometimes too overpowering. All

44

22. *Left :* Costume for Mr. Leslie Banks as Petruchio.
23. *Right :* Costume for Miss Edith Evans as Katharina.

this applies also to coverings of chairs or sofas. Should the furnishings be for a period play, the materials, patterns, trimmings, or shape must assume the character of that period.

The drapery and furniture of a room are the principal allies in helping to give the room an air of the period and in the choice of colour and material an excellent indication of the gaiety or gloom of the production can be given.

Furnishings—like costumes—can be submitted to fantastic treatment provided the characteristics of the period are maintained as a foundation. In such cases the materials used must be regarded as a basis from which to conjure a vivid parody, and trimmings or decorations, equally devoid of all authenticity, can nevertheless portray the essentials of the period in their own way.

25. Design for showgirl in Revue, showing a costume in which it will be necessary to use flesh-coloured net.

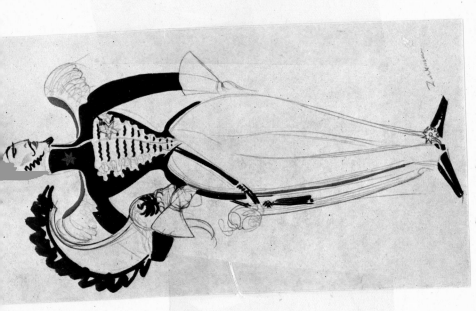

24. Costume for a musical play showing exaggeration of line and conception.

47

CHAPTER 7 PERIOD COSTUME

There have been endless works written on costume and designing costume that go very fully into details regarding each period and give an abundance of information of the variations in costumes in their respective spheres and countries. It is not my aim to go over this ground again, which has been already done most adequately, but rather to advise how to make use of such information.

Many costumes are designed to a chocolate-box semblance of the period they are meant to represent. They are like the paintings of a bad draughtsman who knows little or nothing about anatomy. To be able to appreciate and recognise the points that are the base on which the fashion of every era in turn achieves its character, one should go over each line and contour in an endeavour to discover how the silhouette is built up.

There are in all garments certain eccentricities in cut according to the fashions of the day, which were carefully planned with a view to arriving at a particular outline, and to capture these essential lines by taking the trouble to detect and unravel their mysteries is of far more value in making a costume interesting and beautiful as well as correct than a cartload of magnificent materials. Learning how to look for these vital features so necessary to the outline in all costumes will not only act as a key to many books on the subject, but will also add considerably to the enjoyment of contemporary pictures, in appreciating how the fashionable figure and type of beauty then in vogue creeps into the work of every painter.

For example, if a Victorian artist painted Boadicea charging into battle in a chariot he gave her the sentimental oval face and limpid eyes so much admired in those days. Her clothes, too, would very likely have a distinctly Victorian flavour in their design.

For the purpose of explaining myself more clearly I am taking as an example three different periods where the costumes have similar foundations. Their appearances are altered entirely by a deviation in the cut, making the ultimate result appear to change the shape of the figure in each case.

The silhouette of the period is the most important of all things

26.   Elizabethan picture showing a good example of the Contemporary
silhouette.

(Queen Elizabeth, by an unknown artist.   Reproduced by permission of
the National Portrait Gallery, where it is to be seen.)

to be considered. The reason period costume so often looks like fancy dress on the stage is because there has been positively no attempt to adhere to the original cut and so the silhouette is absent. All too often costumes are made with a mere attempt at outline and garnished with a lot of trimmings (which are also as far removed from the period as the shape of the dress) in an effort to make them look what is known as " Old World."

The two most popular and most maligned periods are Early Victorian and Georgian. I have known a costumier use the same dress for either period when hiring out for productions. A few bows down the front of the bodice made it Georgian, and with the addition of a bit of lace round the neck, some rosebuds in posies sprinkled about, and a hooped petticoat underneath the skirt, it was transformed into the sort of Early Victorian costume one too often sees, which is uninteresting and totally lacking in charm. With so many wonderful contemporary portraits and pictures there should never be any excuse for incorrect silhouettes.

Bodies have not changed in shape ; only the fashions in figure change according to the amount of plumpness or slimness that happens to be in vogue. And slim or plump, there invariably must be many who are unfashionable. The portrait painters in each era have always very discreetly added a little plumpness where necessary or reduced unfortunate generosity of line.

It is the cut of the clothes that gives the very misleading structural alteration to the appearance of the figure. Take as an example the Early Victorian silhouette. Wasp waists and sloping shoulders are the most striking feature of this period.

The idea that women suddenly developed bottle shoulders or that their waists dwindled is a fallacy. The silhouette is made only by the line and cut of the clothes. " Ah," you say, " but they *had* slim waists, and lovely dimpled shoulders. My grandmother had the tiniest waist, measuring only seventeen inches." This may be perfectly correct, but do not forget that for your one beautiful fashionably-shaped grandmother there were forty other grand-mothers with enormous waists and horribly unfashionable figures, as any family album will show. The corset of the day certainly helped, but only to some extent. To-day, for every lovely slim long-legged Ginger Rogers, there are a hundred diet-eating

50

VICTORIAN

GEORGIAN

ELIZABETHAN

27. Three silhouettes showing the variation in the line of the bodice.

wretches who rush to beauty specialists for slimming baths in an attempt to attain the silhouette of the moment.

Look at an Early Victorian fashion plate and see how every line in the bodice is designed to produce sloping shoulders and tiny waists. The sleeve line is set not on the shoulder but just below with all fullness and trimmings beneath that again, to help to accentuate the long shoulder line. Designs vary, but they are all cut to exaggerate this trend in fashion. The décolletage of an evening gown follows the same line and is worn just on the point of the shoulder. Should it slip down or be worn (entirely incorrectly) lower, it will immediately result in making the shoulders look square. The rest of the lines of the bodice together with a full skirt contrive to make the waist look small. Deviate from these lines and you have lost the Early Victorian figure.

Compare the lines of the Georgian bodice with that of the Early Victorian, taking the most typical shape running through the Georgian era. It was an altogether much longer, straighter, less sentimental, and more voluptuous affair. The décolletage began high up, fitting closely round the back of the neck, gradually curving outwards down the front, taking the line of the bosom and forming a most attractive and seductive shape. Another neckline was square, which went even further towards giving the straighter appearance, and this, together with the stomacher, a panel so often down the front of a Georgian bodice, and the tendency to push the bosom up higher, added to the illusion of greater length.

The Elizabethan bodice is even longer and straighter in appearance. In this the bosom is pushed up until it is almost at right angles and the end of the stomacher comes well down below the waistline in front, giving tremendous length, though at the back the bodice itself only reaches the actual waistline. Sometimes these Elizabethan bodices have slung sleeves—magnificent things that pile high above the shoulders on either side and look as if they were inflated. Queen Elizabeth seemed to prefer this fashion to the many alternatives of her day, and, though she was a very thin woman in nearly all portraits of her, the figure, as it stands, could be placed into a square, the width of the sleeves being almost the same as that of the hem of the skirt.

28. A Georgian silhouette.

(The Marquise de Pompadour, by Boucher.
From the picture in the Wallace Collection, by
permission.)

Whether dealing with men's or women's costumes, I cannot place too much emphasis on this question of silhouette.

In the choice of materials, these should be in character with the period and any form of stuff may be used provided it produces that character. Costumes that must be essentially realistic should be made of materials as near to those used in the period as possible. Where licence may be taken and imagination allowed to run free, materials of the most outrageous contradiction can be made to conform to any period.

In the decoration of a costume astonishing results may emerge from thought and invention and in many cases the best effects are produced through the use of materials that are quite peculiarly foreign to the purposes to which they are put. Designs may be embroidered, painted or *appliqué* on the groundwork, but the period must be preserved in all designs and patterns, however fantastic. Such trimmings that form part of the costume should imitate even to exaggeration those of the period; in fact, in most instances these trimmings are more effective and delightful when rather caricatured.

Lace is a material that can be wonderfully improvised with a little ingenuity, and anyway, it is always difficult to get lace that is right in character. Take, as an instance, a cravat in the time of Charles II. I have seen a paper doily used to far greater advantage than any lace procurable; and His Majesty was able to have a new one for every performance!

Fashions for August. 1844.

29.   Victorian silhouettes.

CHAPTER 8   COSTUME EN MASSE

Large numbers of figures together present a problem that requires a rather special treatment. Whether in groups where there are several in the same costume, or in a crowd that consists of many varied costumes, or maybe in a line of Chorus, they should at first all be thought of as scenery. But always simplicity and economy of line and colour are most effective. Some of the best examples to be found anywhere are in the costumes and colour groupings of the Russian Ballet, which are generally superbly simple in design.

For instance, a scene called " The Waltz," from the ballet " Symphonie Fantastique," carries out these principles to perfection. All the ladies are in creamy white costumes of 1830, and the gentlemen in black evening dress of the period, giving tremendous value to the beautiful and perfectly-thought-out setting of tier upon tier of bright crimson arches against a very thundery sky of battleship grey. Here is the use of only four colours producing a lovely picture that is completely satisfying.

Having been thought of primarily as scenery, the figures should next evolve into a costume design, but though one design may stand for two or twenty costumes, it must be such that it only comes into its own by being repeated. The weight of colour in these groups of repeat costumes should be carefully planned, always with a view to the costumes of the principal characters in the scene who must on no account be confused with any of the Chorus in their appearance. A principal must always stand out whether he or she is dressed in the most magnificent costume or merely in rags. A line of Chorus is very often dressed in one design repeated, and is generally more effective when the design is simple.

Chorus girls are easy to design for, charming to deal with and always pleased when given nice clothes to wear on the stage. Try to please the people who are to wear your costumes and they will always look at their best in them.

Costume for dancing must be designed so that it looks equally well in movement or motionless. It must also remain intact all through the performance of the wearer, no matter how strenuous.

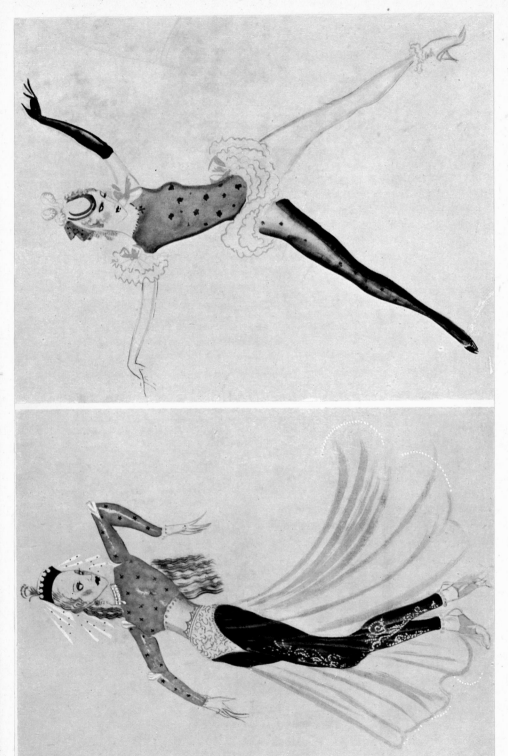

30. Costume for Revue worn by a chorus of eight girls.   31. Costume design used for a chorus of twenty-four girls.

It is the fault of the designer if a costume is so badly thought out that it impedes the movements in any way and it is unpardonable if any part of a costume comes adrift or falls off during a performance.

It is always a pleasure to design clothes for the showgirls, the mannequins of the stage. Chosen for their tall, slender figures they do not—thank heaven !—possess those anatomical peculiarities, so often disfiguring their more eminent colleagues, which are beyond the power of man to conceal.

In crowd scenes, such as streets or assemblies, in which everyone is dressed differently, greater value and far more brilliance of colour are achieved by designing at least twenty-five per cent. of the costumes in rather quiet, sombre colours as a contrast to the brighter ones.

The use of a certain proportion of black and white is always of value when there are a number of colours together. There was a time when white was taboo on the stage and such articles as collars, cuffs, table-linen, etc., were dipped in tea or made of ecru-coloured material. My own view is that the use of white is essential in decoration, and that it looks as well on the stage as it does anywhere else.

Oliver Messel has made use of white more effectively than anyone, and has designed whole scenes that are entirely white. His setting for the bedroom in " Helen " is, to my mind, one of the best examples of his work, brilliantly clever and an extremely beautiful scene.

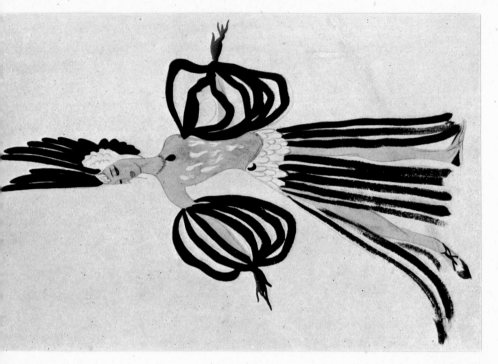

33. Costume for showgirl.

32. Costume showing 1900 silhouette.

59

CH: 9 COSTUME IN THE MAKING

The actual drawing-out of a costume does not in itself present serious difficulties. In fact, there is considerable enjoyment to be derived from the making of an attractive drawing, apart from the thinking out of the idea and the use of colour to obtain an effect. The real difficulties arise in the carrying-out of the design, and the secret of achieving satisfactory results is to know exactly what you want before you start.

A costume should be thought of as a finished production as far as possible before it is committed to paper. In thinking out the shape of each part—jacket, trousers, bodice, waistcoat, skirt, etc.— decide upon the material of which each garment is to be made. To have all these points clearly defined means knowing what you want when it comes to instructing the costumier in carrying out the design. Choosing materials should be done very largely under artificial light as certain stuffs react differently to colour when subjected to these lights.

There are also materials of a thin, gauzy nature that may look anything but transparent under certain lighting effects, and these should always be tried in preparation. Satins are the most likely to keep their colour, silks are also fairly reliable, but velvets require to be tried under stage lighting as they change very much, especially the dark colours. Cloth, too, should be handled with care in the darker shades. Cotton materials may be relied on to keep their colour pretty well, but there are certain shades in every type of stuff that change very considerably in stage lighting.

Patterns of every material that is to be used in making a costume should be chosen and passed as satisfactory before the costumier is allowed to proceed in his work. The designer should see samples of all trimmings, buttons, flowers, feathers, and so on. Should any of these have to be specially dyed, select a pattern of the colour for dyeing so that there shall be no mistake.

Always give a diagram for special ornamentation on a costume or for anything that is likely to be confusing to the dressmaker.

Opposite :
34 (above). Design for " Spanish Melody " scene in " Happy Returns." 35 (below). The actual scene, with dancers. The designs for the costumes of the pair on the right are on p. 63.

A description of the costume will probably be necessary in spite of giving a clear, understandable drawing, as a conscientious dressmaker is always anxious to interpret all that is in the design as correctly as possible.

The details of cut and line should be gone into as well as the practicability of making. Where exaggeration is required in the cutting of a period costume the designer should be doubly careful in his explanations. An old experienced fitter will no doubt have very fixed views on what he or she considers to be correct, and it is as well to point out very clearly from the beginning how these exaggerations shall be carried out.

Costumes for a revue often appear to have been blown on to the girls who are wearing them, and you wonder by what means the little amount of costume there is ever stays in place. Most dresses of this type are made on a very well-fitting foundation of flesh-coloured net. The net is specially fine and very strong as most dresses of this nature in revue are used for dancing numbers. In designing one of these rather nude affairs it is always more effective if, where the net terminates, one contrives that part of the more solid material in the costume divides the bare skin from that which is covered with net. Solid portions, while dutifully making it possible for the costume to pass the Censor, should be used to cover up such joins in the net foundation that might spoil the illusion of nudity.

All fittings of costumes should be attended to and errors in cut and making corrected there and then. There are nearly always final adjustments to be made to one or two costumes at the Dress Parade, but one should work hard in an endeavour to produce everything completed as far as possible by that time.

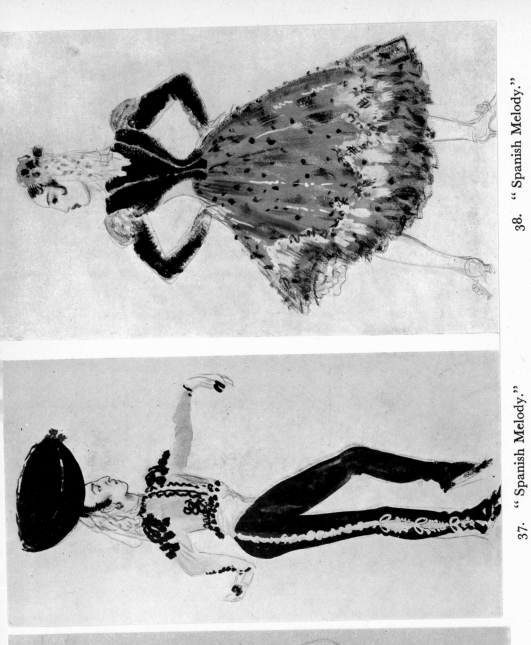

36. "Highland Swing."   37. "Spanish Melody."   38. "Spanish Melody."

Three costumes for individuals in "Happy Returns."

CH: 10 WIGS AND HAIRDRESSING

The head is of the greatest importance as it is subjected to more concentrated scrutiny than any other part, especially in these days of designing for films, where there are so many " close-ups."

Wigs can be perfect, and there are some superb wigmakers who can make toupees, beards, wigs, etc., that are impossible to detect.

The cleverest example of this art I think I have ever seen was a transformation worn by a young, though very bald, man, who is a well-known and extremely brilliant dancer. He has appeared in Cochran shows and many times in cabaret. Nobody, however close to him, could have told that he had not got a perfectly groomed head of hair, and he did a most vigorous dancing act, at times swinging his partner round his head ; yet still the wig remained secure and perfect.

In most wigs the average wigmaker uses hair which is too coarse. This sort of hair is too springy and consequently difficult to dress neatly. Others will use too much hair in a wig, making it look bundly and giving the wearer a big clumsy head. The worst examples of this type are to be seen in performances done by amateur societies, though I have seen some very startling ones on the professional stage.

With costumes where hair requires dressing in the manner of the period, or in certain cases when a wig is worn, the silhouette of the hair is just as important as that of the costume. All too often a beautiful costume will be completely ruined by the wearer being permitted to appear with her own modern coiffure and perhaps a few added curls at the back to give the idea of being in some sort of alliance with the costume. This is an unpardonable crime and should be fought against at all costs.

Just as occasions call for fantasy in costumes, so it will occur in hairdressing and wigs, and there is a marvellous opportunity to let imagination run riot in creating something that has all the conformation and line of a perfectly dressed coiffure, without anything so commonplace as a single hair being used in its construction. There have been some very lovely and very clever wigs made of very strange things—materials such as wire, felt, tinfoil,

64

glass, silk braid, horsehair, cellophane—in fact, anything that will produce the necessary effect of hair in caricature. In designing this type of fantastic wig it is even more important than usual to give clear readable sketches and diagrams, and also to remember that the wigmaker who can make a perfectly natural wig has not always the flair or aptitude for making a fantastic one.

And even when one has done everything possible to ensure the correctness of the wigs for a show, it still remains to see that the cast put them on and wear them correctly. I can remember revisiting a show which I had designed, about a fortnight after the opening, to discover one of the chorus girls wearing her wig back to front with perfect equanimity.

39. An actual pair of Victorian boots.

They are made of a cloth material and are cut to fit the foot like a glove. This photograph shows that it is possible to make feet look like those of any Victorian fashion picture.

CHAPTER 11 SHOES AND HATS

Shoes can be so lovely, boots so interesting; and yet how often is the amount of trouble taken that is really due to either of them?

The study of contemporary pictures of any period will prove, on examining the feet, to be full of all sorts of fantastic, charming and humorous features that are not only part but add to the interest and beauty of the costume.

The silhouette of the shoe is the most difficult part of a costume to have carried out to any degree of satisfaction. The makers of period shoes generally become paralysed when asked to make anything that does not conform to their usual stock patterns, which are very limited. The only way to achieve any result approaching the design is to have a clear idea, and a still clearer drawing, with every help in the way of diagrams.

Leading ladies are often difficult about period shoes and would prefer to wear a pair of high-heeled slippers from Bond Street, a procedure which it is hardly necessary to suggest should be resisted to the death.

If the designer has exercised judgment in evolving a particular costume, and has taken the trouble to get the line and the details correct, it is hardly likely that such an important accessory as the hat will have been neglected, for the whole effect can be made or marred by a hat which is out of period, unsuitable or badly worn. Yet I have frequently seen a hat complacently worn above a dress which was fifty years later in period, and investigation has generally disclosed a principal who fancied herself under a wide brim, over-riding all objections.

However great the temptation may sometimes be to envelop and camouflage as much as possible of some particularly unattractive actress, it should always be borne in mind that, in the same way that a dress may have to be designed to give freedom for dancing, a hat must never interfere with its wearer's acting, and it must at all times be correct, comfortable and secure.

Examples
of
Modern Stage
Design
discussed

The Taming of the Shrew

DESIGNED BY DORIS ZINKEISEN

THE BANQUET

This is a photograph of the scene of which
the frontispiece shows the model. Considered with the illustrations on the next
page, it demonstrates how, in a Shakespearian production, the same scene can,
by the alteration of backcloths and small
set pieces, be adapted to serve for various
interiors and exteriors, as described on
page 26.

40

The Taming of the Shrew

THE BANQUET

The Taming of the Shrew

THE ROAD TO PADUA

A change of backcloth sets the scene in the country.

For interiors, either curtains were drawn behind the pillars, or a small inset scene was set behind the central arch of the pillars, the remaining two being masked with the curtains that ran behind.

For exteriors, either a cloth and wings or set pieces were used, or in the case of one illustration, a bookwing either side and a flat in the central arch.

42

The Taming of the Shrew

OUTSIDE LUCENTIO'S HOUSE

A new backcloth sets the scene in city streets.

Scene from " Helen "

BY OLIVER MESSEL

Oliver Messel's design for the bedroom scene in " Helen." Entirely in white, a colour considered at one time impossible for stage use, this scene was brilliantly successful.

This was a semi-circular scene, consisting of soft draperies with a pillow either side of the stage.

The bed itself was circular, which half fitted into the recess, as seen in the illustration, and was decorated by a Cupid and two gigantic swans. The *pièce de résistance* was the overhanging lamp, from which came four thin white draperies. They gave to an already transparent, filmy scene the effect of unreality.

Oliver Messel handles light and delicate colours better than almost any designer for the stage.

43.   *Design for scene in " Helen " by Oliver Messel.*

44

Backcloth from " Happy Returns "

BY DORIS ZINKEISEN

Design for a backcloth, used as a background for a dancing number. The curtains were painted in deep crimson, and the little vista in delicate greys and pinks. Against this cloth, the chorus of dancers wore turquoise-blue dresses trimmed with touches of black and cut on simple very severe lines.

The lighting for this scene, unlike the usual dancing number, which has generally a flood of light over the whole stage, was in strong contrasts of light and shadow. The figures were lit from one side only, and the cloth had just a glimmer of red to give depth to the colour.

44. *Backcloth from " Happy Returns " by Doris Zinkeisen.*

45

Backcloth for Jungle Number in " Happy Returns "

BY DORIS ZINKEISEN

This cloth is the setting for a very wild native dancing number. This design was for a set in which it was necessary to convey the spirit of the scene on a cloth, without the assistance of wings, borders, or set pieces, as the stage was entirely masked in at the sides by curtains.

The jungle was mostly in varying shades of greens, the trunks of the trees either black or very dark brown, and the tiger in a greeny gold.

The costumes were made of horsehair, having short skirts in a very brilliant pink, springing from a girdle of gold embroidery encrusted with huge rubies the size of eggs.

The wigs were black and white horsehair, spraying out on top of the head rather like a sweep's brush, and surmounted by two huge quills. The dancers also wore many bracelets made of ivory and some of gold with tiny balls dangling from them, which made a savage jingling noise as they moved.

The principal dancer wore a girdle of gold embroidery and huge black feathers. Her headdress was gold with horns coming from the temples on either side, and tall shining quills ranging from short at the back of the head, following the line of the parting, to very tall ones on the forehead.

45.   *Design for Jungle Number in " Happy Returns," by Doris Zinkeisen.*

*Design for " The Ball " in " Symphonie
Fantastique "*

BY CHRISTIAN BÉRARD

A wonderful scene in an unbelievable economy of colours. For sheer beauty of design and originality in conception, at the same time conveying the atmosphere of the period, I have rarely seen anything to equal this on the stage.

Christian Bérard's designs for the new ballet " Seventh Symphony " are exceptionally beautiful. As in " Symphonie Fantastique," for his scenes he uses nothing but backcloths and cut cloths, with occasionally a set piece consisting of gigantic figures in the form of pillars. The scenes are very simple in design and form a perfect balance of colour with the costumes.

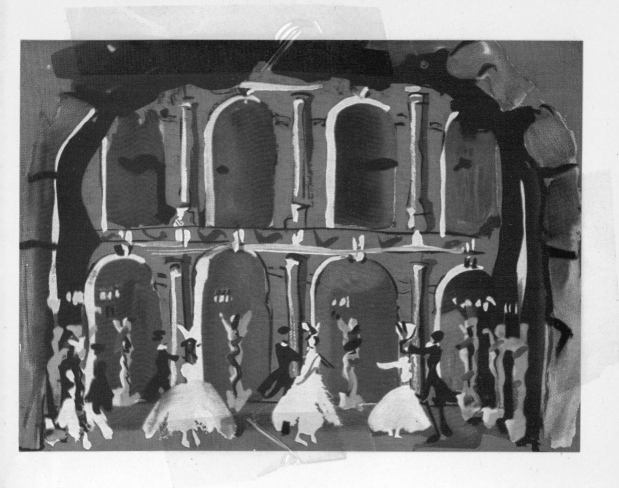

46

*Design for " The Ball" in "Symphonie
Fantastique"*

BY CHRISTIAN BÉRARD